Pun Day in Your Life

A Journal to the Centre of the Mirth

Paul Eggleston

Copyright © 2021 Paul Eggleston

All rights reserved.

No part of this book may be reproduced, or stored in a retrieval system, or transmitted in any form or by any means, electronic, mechanical, photocopying, recording, or otherwise, without express written permission of the publisher.

ISBN: 9798766149354

DEDICATION

To Jodi, Ruby & Ethan, and all my family and friends, who have to put up with this sort of thing all the time.

To my dearly missed Father, who didn't get to hear many of my jokes, but whose sense of humour I inherited. I think he would have chuckled at some of this book. Probably not *all* of it though.

To everyone who's been so kind to me over the years on Twitter.

...and to the best cats in the world, Cookie and Crumble, because Ruby will never forgive me if I don't mention them (they're also on the front cover now and, look, they've snuck in here too!)

PREFACE

Ever since I was very young, I would think up silly puns and jokes. Not necessarily always entirely original concepts, but they came out of my own head. It just seems to be the way I'm wired. The earliest one that I remember making people laugh with was 'What do they call the cleverest sister in the convent? Nun the wiser!', or words to that effect. I must have been about 9 or 10. It's not my strongest material, but I still occasionally think of nun-puns (as you will see) so feel free to insert a joke about habits here.

I first ventured onto Twitter in 2009 on the recommendation of a friend, not really knowing what it was all about, and not having anything particularly interesting to say (not much has changed there). And then I found hashtag games which, for the uninitiated, involve thinking up ridiculous puns on a theme… and it felt like I'd come home.

Twitter became a focus for my punning energy, and I started becoming more prolific, and spending time honing my tweets. I wince now at my early efforts (as many doubtless wince at my current efforts!), but I learnt what worked as I wrote, both from the instant feedback (in the form of retweets, likes, and replies saying 'groan' and the like – which I always take as a compliment) and from the amazing people I have met through Twitter over the years.

I do think the character limit on Twitter has helped too, in a funny sort of way (it used to be 140 characters you know, back when it was all fields!) It's meant having to draft and redraft tweets and in some cases you really have to make every single character count. Even with the current 280 character limit it can be a struggle to construct a set-up to a particularly convoluted wordplay. Though, at the other end of the spectrum, very brief jokes can be quite satisfying too.

The shortest one I've ever written is:

,dAu

It's only four characters but, my goodness, it's comedy gold.

My style *can* be quite divisive. I seem to have a reputation for high convolution 'brain pretzels' which can elicit praise and borderline threatening behaviour in equal measure, and I do enjoy the challenge of those. They're sometimes as challenging to work out as they are to write - often likened to getting a cryptic crossword clue (pro tip: try saying the pun out loud in a variety of different regional accents). I'm quite partial to a pithy one-liner too, but I so often find those have been done before, in some shape or form, which is what tends to push me back to the mental acrobatics.

I do try to be as 'family friendly' as possible. There might be a couple of *mildly* rude words in this book, and a smattering of toilet humour, but that's pretty much as bad as I get. Though, out of interest, what do you think the sleaziest way of disguising four multiple choice options as one is? Is it:

a) be seedy

Over the years a few people have suggested that I write a book, and as I appear to have accumulated quite a bit of material I thought now seemed like a good time. I suppose it's nice to think that in years to come, when Twitter isn't a thing any more, someone might pick up and peruse a copy of this book and scratch their head, saying 'East Hippo Park have a leak...?' over and over again wondering what the hell that's supposed to mean (well not that *actual* pun, I thought I'd be kind and leave that one out, but it is available on Twitter).

I decided to put it into a sort of diary format because a) it's something different; b) it gives me something to aim for i.e. 365 puns, give or take, and c) It's meant I can try to give it a bit of a seasonal flavour. That does however mean the eagle-eyed reader might spot some continuity errors:

> 'Hang on, your children were TINY last week and now they seem to be all grown up!
>
> 'Exactly how many weird pets DO you have?'
>
> 'How many jobs HAVE you had in ONE YEAR?'
>
> 'Where DO you find the time for all those weird genetic engineering experiments?'
>
> 'You do MAKE some weird decisions on WHICH words to CAPITALISE.'

In some cases – full disclosure here – it might just look a bit like a pun with a date above it - but I suppose it helps with the word count.

When push comes to shove, the thing that motivated me to put this convolution compendium together (and that will always bring me back to Twitter) is hoping that I can make someone, somewhere (anyone?) laugh. But I'll always settle for a groan.

PROLOGUE

Captain Superheroic Mouse (his name was a mouthful, but it avoided any potential copyright issues) was flying along, minding his own super-business, when his super-hearing picked up a distant yell. "CHEESE!" came the cry. Intrigued, and a little hungry, he flew towards the sound. He arrived at a treacle factory, of all things. "CHEESE!" he heard again, from an open window, so he flew in.

"CHEESE!"

The sound was coming from a vat of treacle. He peered in and saw an elderly lady mouse struggling to stay afloat. Quick as a flash he pulled her out of danger and took her to safety.

"Thank you, Captain Superheroic Mouse!" she said. "I live in this factory, and I fell in the vat when I was on my way to the mouse youth club downstairs. All the little ones there see me as a grandmother figure."

"You Nana Mouse?" asked our hero.

"Yes, every single one of them agrees. I really do appreciate you saving me."

"No problem, Ma'am. But can I ask why you were shouting 'CHEESE!'?"

"Well I was shouting 'HELP!' for ages but you didn't hear. I thought cheese might get your attention!"

"Fair enough. You take care now," said Captain Superheroic Mouse, and off he flew.

The next day Captain Superheroic Mouse was flying along once more, when again he heard a distant shout of "CHEESE!". He went to investigate, perplexed. Sure enough it was the treacle factory again. "CHEESE!" a little voice yelled, so in he went.

"CHEESE!"

The sound was coming from the same vat of treacle. This time he saw a young male mouse fighting for his life, so as fast as a… er… small rodent with super-rodent powers, he grabbed him from the jaws of treacly doom.

"Thank you, Captain Superheroic Mouse!" he said. "I live in this factory, and I fell in the vat when I was getting some shopping for my wife. She's pregnant you see, and growing by the day."

"Bigger mouse?" he replied.

"No, I only have one wife. Thanks for rescuing me."

"It's all good. But why did you shout 'CHEESE'?"

"Well the lady you saved yesterday said it worked!"

"Oh, OK. Stay safe now!" said Captain Superheroic Mouse,

heroically, and away he soared.

The next day Captain Superheroic Mouse was on patrol and, sure enough, he heard a cry of "CHEESE!" again. Slightly annoyed now, he followed the sound back to the treacle factory and flew in.

"CHEESE!"

Again he peered in the same vat of treacle, and this time saw an older male mouse gasping for breath. Still super-quickly, but without quite the same urgency as before, he dragged the mouse to dry land.

"Thank you, Captain Superheroic Mouse!" he said. "I live in this factory, and I fell in the vat when I was on my way to the royal mouse palace, to be knighted by the mouse queen!"

"Is that an honour, mouse?" Captain Superheroic Mouse inquired.

"No, she knows my name. Cheers for saving my life, though!"

"No worries. Though I'm getting a bit annoyed with everyone shouting 'CHEESE!' to get my attention."

"Well after the last couple of days, it's now very specific official mouse advice. If you fall in a vat of treacle, shout 'CHEESE!' and Captain Superheroic Mouse will save you."

Our heroic rodent looked dejected. His rescuee started flickering his paw in the treacle.

"What are you doing?" asked Captain Superheroic Mouse.

"You don't look very happy so I just thought I'd try fluttering molasses at you."

Off flew Captain Superheroic Mouse, sighing, into the sunset.

Now I take no pleasure in summarising this story with a tortuous wordplay, but if you have been affected by any of the puns in this story, and if you become affected by any of the terrible puns that will follow in this book, I would like to offer you 'mice in syrup holler 'CHEESE!''

Just to set the tone for the rest of the book (it's not *that* bad)…

JANUARY

1ˢᵗ January

Happy New Year!

Decided that I will keep a diary this year.

Never done it before!

Apart from that time that I started to keep a journal of all the indifferent kisses that I received.

Though I never got round to publishing my 'meh' mwahs.

2ⁿᵈ January

Just spoke to an officer doing door to door enquiries.

Apparently a man has been seen acting suspiciously near a bird enclosure at the local convent.

Sounds like a nun's aviary character to me.

3rd January

Amazing personal achievement today!

I officiated a spelling bee years ago, and asked the contestant to spell 'leniency'.

He asked if I could use it in a sentence.

So I got a law degree, worked in law and became a judge.

And today – FINALLY - I let a robber off with a £1 fine.

4th January

Went to Hannibal Lecter's birthday party today!

I met some really fun people dressed as volcano monsters, and Hannibal's uncle's wife who enjoys nocturnal winter sports!

I made him a cake. He ate a sliver with some lava beings and a night ski auntie.

5th January

Had to go to the hospital earlier, and get an X-ray of my leg.

The doctor said, "Your patella measures 2.54cm".

I said, "Inch-high knees?"

He said, "您的髌骨是2.54厘米高."

6th January

The DVD player went a bit weird today.

I tried to watch 'The Omen', but it would only play backwards, which was a shame.

Though I did end up Finding Nemo.

7th January

We've finally moved into our new home!

We're renting a house from the matron at the local ursine hospital, and it's full of inflatable sofas.

It doesn't sound great, but it's got all the bear nurse air settees.

8th January

Our new neighbourhood seems lovely!

The neighbour on one side has a green triangular house. On the other side it's an orange octagon.

I live in a quality street!

9th January

Met Tom Jones today. Lovely chap.

He made me a cheese and marmalade sandwich! There's only one word to describe how it tasted:

CHEESEALADEY!

Whoa whoa whoa!

10th January

Ugh. Had to do some DIY today.

There were a lot of gaps in between the bathroom tiles, but I didn't know what to fill them with.

So I just used a load of Frosties, mushed up with milk to form a paste.

They're grrrrrrrout!

11th January

Went out for a meal this evening.

I told the waiter that the Hollandaise tasted funny - he said that was because it was 'lol-landaise'.

Which was a sauce of amusement.

12th January

I was just chewing my biro as I was wondering what to write, and got to thinking that I don't really know what I'd do if a pen leaked in my mouth.

I dread tooth ink!

13th January

Went for a job interview this afternoon.

The interviewer said, "Can I ask you to tell me why you want the job, in just three words?"

I said, "Of course".

So he said, "Why want job?"

14th January

Lovely christening today.

Though unfortunately the priest used the wrong kind of font, so now the poor kid is a Times New Roman Catholic.

15th January

Went to a comic book convention this afternoon.

I was chatting to a friend, when this bloke rudely interrupted me just to list off each actor who's played The Hulk, and how tall they were.

Which was the height of mad Banners!

16th January

Just got off the phone to Cliff Richard!

He wants to buy my recording of the 'Lord of the Rings' author describing a brief stroll through a valley in Middle-earth.

He's got himself acquiring Tolkien's fleeting walk in Rivendell.

17th January

Went to see a friend today.

He asked me to make him a dinner set, even though my pottery skills are limited to creating oversized bowls, so I'm not sure he's really thought it through.

But I might be doing him a huge dish service.

18th January

Had to quickly nip over to New York today!

I find American law so confusing. I was arrested for kneeling down and pretending I was a unicorn, but I'm not sure if that's a myth demeanour or a fell on knee?

19th January

Just popped out for a coffee, and I can't find my instructions for how sheets of paper are made into a book.

They're bound to be a tome.

20th January

I've rented the stuff
for the poets' party. It's
the leased haiku do.

21st January

Amazing news!

Just heard that my friend has got out of prison after serving a sentence for robbing a train that was pulling a fabled buffet car stocked with only frozen water.

He definitely didn't do it though.

It was a myth carriage of just ice.

22nd January

My wife and I renewed our wedding vows this afternoon.

I think she only married me for my electric whisk and my large jug.

For beater, for whirrs. For pitcher, for pourer.

23rd January

All been a bit stressful today.

I had to phone Anagramaholics Anonymous to rearrange my appointment.

They suggested 'Minty Pant Poem'.

24th January

Darts practice this evening!

Just found out that my new coach is a Mother Superior who's booked a holiday in Port-au-Prince but has a phobia of flying.

ONE NUN DREADING HAITI!

25th January

You'll never believe what I saw when I was waiting in line for Queen tickets today!

@pauleggleston

26ᵗʰ January

Met a duck this afternoon, while I was doing the crossword.

I asked it what the capital city of Canada is.

It said, "Quack, Ottawa," but I thought that was a volcanic island in Indonesia?

27ᵗʰ January

A very challenging day today.

All my pet weasel did was donate some money to a little dog for his charity drumming marathon, and now he's been accused of stoat sponsored terrier rhythm.

28ᵗʰ January

Had to go to the doctors today.

This bloke was walking around in a white coat, blowing loudly on a goose whistle.

I think he must have been the honk call doctor.

29th January

Couldn't sleep last night.

My gopher / dachshund cross-breeding project is running a little low on money at the moment.

So I've just been setting up a new GophundMe page.

30th January

Just back from the shops.

I bought a new raincoat for our rabbit. I wasn't sure about it, but it came with a bunny mac guarantee.

31st January

My wife's going out tonight.

She reckons she's going to a Rudyard Kipling poetry themed fancy-dress party.

As If!

FEBRUARY

To my darling Valentine,

Roses are red,
Violets are blue,
I love the way snails
Exude trails of goo!

love,
your secrete admirer xxx

@pauleggleston

1st February

> Trouble at work today!!
>
> The macaw that lives on my office workspace has irritated several different Frenchmen with its glockenspiel.
>
> I don't know what they're going to do about it.
>
> But desk parrot chimes gall four disparate messieurs.

2nd February

> SO BORED of applying for jobs. Spent all day on it!
>
> Though I'm pretty confident in my application to work at the spaghetti hoops factory, as I have a canned ooo attitude.

3rd February

> Tried to cheer up our pet weasel this afternoon by tying him to a balloon and flying him so high that he could see all the fêtes in the local area, but it didn't work.
>
> It was a very sad stoat over fairs.

4th February

Saw a social media post about the Crewe to Holyhead train line today. It was really popular.

It went via Rhyl!

5th February

Word has got out that I'm writing a diary, and there seems to be a rumour doing the rounds that I'm being paid to promote German filled pastry within it. I'd just like to confirm that this isn't the case.

It looks like something must just have been misconstrudel.

6th February

I heard a lost verse from a Beatles song today:

> *One of my grannies*
> *Smelt a bit musty and bought milk in bottles each day,*
> *Got put away.*
> *The other grandmother*
> *Smelt more of citrus and bought milk in boxes instead,*
> *She is now dead.*

It was from 'Eleanor Rigby', by Lemon Nan More Cartony.

7th February

Bumped into Elton John this morning.

He was telling me that apparently, in the middle ages, if mounted soldiers needed a poo they had to do it in their armour because it was so difficult to take off.

They weren't happy about it, but it didn't put them off.

Because sad turdy knight's alright for fighting.

8th February

Very impressed with the local police service today!

I called for help because I found that bloke from Luther struggling to cover his own head in gift paper.

They immediately sent out the Wrap Idris Bonce Unit.

9th February

Games night this evening!!

I just played 'DINGDONG' in a game of Scrabble.

I got a doorbell word score!

10th February

Nightmare!

We got burgled last night, and I saw the chap who did it.

I went to the police station and the officer said, "Can you identify the screwdriver used by the burglar from these ten pictures? And his headwear from these ten?"

I said, "It's tool eight, fourth hat".

Then he said, "We won't catch him with that defeatist attitude, sir."

11th February

Just off to get my antique lint roller valued.

Apparently it's a collect hairs item.

12th February

I bought a coat in a charity shop today. It once belonged to Louis Armstrong!

He even wrote a song about it, that I found in the pocket!

> *I see coat of wool*
> *And toggles too*
> *It keeps me warm*
> *Wish I had two*
> *And I think to myself*
> *What a one duffle world...*

13th February

My wife just put on a Gregorian Monks CD, and started flicking through a magazine, which made me feel a bit uneasy!

I never like to leaf anything to chants.

14th February

Ahhh, Valentine's Day!

I think 'bouquet' is a more romantic word than 'bunch'.

At least that's what I'll be telling my wife when I give her a bouquet of bananas later.

15th February

Just back from the hypnotist.

I want him to hypnotise our cat to think it's a dog, but he said, "I'm afraid there's only a 50% chance that it will sound like one."

"I regret two in four mew."

16th February

Just catching up with the news.

Apparently a truckload of E45 has overturned on its way to Sam from Cheers' house

Agnetha from ABBA happened to be passing, so was helping to clear up the mess with a shovel.

See that girl. Watch that scene. Diggin' the Danson cream!

17th February

Just knocked on the neighbour's door to ask if she'd seen a missing chicken belonging to the lady who looks after our kids when we go out.

She said, "Seen your sitter's hen?" but she's actually in her twenties.

18th February

Just back from church!

The minister is getting a bit grumpy about the congregation all sitting on the right, leaving the opposite pews empty in the vicinity of the annoying organist who keeps playing the same Musical Youth song.

Pastor touchy on the left-hand side.

19th February

I really felt like pampering myself today.

I remarked that I've not had a tea enema for years.

My wife said, "Far too long?"

So I said, "No, but I did squeak out some darjeeling once."

20th February

I was set upon in the street earlier!

But a bashful alpaca who works in silvery-white metal extraction came to my rescue.

My shy tin-mining llama!

21st February

Ahhhhh!

I like nothing more than popping a few drops of food colouring into my large pet snake's mineral water.

I feel like I've dyed anaconda Evian.

22nd February

What the hell? A blue police box has just appeared in my house!

A very strange person has emerged and is asking if I'd tie their shoelace, but I'm so busy I can't help.

Knot for the time being.

23rd February

Went to see my mate this morning. He is UNBELIEVABLE.

His mother has always wanted to go and see the Great Barrier Reef, but he's just bought a ticket to go on his own!

Honestly, that bloke has got no coral mum-pass.

24th February

Just been daydreaming!

I was wondering about the chances of Eminem communicating with a Mother Superior over walkie talkies.

If I'm honest it's probably Slim to nun.

25th February

Watching a documentary about the 50s. Love it.

They showed a picture of Hank Marvin before he joined his group. He looked like a former of his Shadow self.

26th February

Went shopping today.

I'm sure I saw a lady who used to groom me in my previous life as a horse. I didn't speak to her though.

She just brushed 'past me'.

27th February

Just on the phone to the police.

Someone came into my garden and deliberately snapped the support for the cord that I peg my washing out on, and I wanted to know what to do.

They asked me to hold the line for a minute but my arm is really aching now.

28th February

Saw a great film today!

It was in the 'action movie star likes to clean his shelves by himself, wearing nothing but a Naval Commandos singlet' genre.

I think it might be my favourite 'SEAL vest, dust alone' film so far!

(Incidentally, I think the Stallone children are the best things since Sly's bred.)

MARCH

12.5% OF BABY SHEEP ARE BORN WITH A PROTECTIVE PLASTIC LAYER, WHICH IS A LAMINATE.....

@pauleggleston

1st March

I went out and bought a Thesaurus today

I regret to say I'm very disappointed with it.

Well, there's no other word for it.

2nd March

Just found out that my neighbour has died. RIP.

He once told his wife that he was just popping out to get some thread but actually went to the pub for the day.

Gone, but not for cotton.

3rd March

Off today, so I read the paper this morning.

Apparently Ronan Keating is taking out a super-injunction to stop the press reporting that he sometimes finds hot cans of Pepsi in his oven.

His wife is a cola roaster, just gotta hide it!

4th March

Just saw a picture on the news of that 'Rolling in the Deep' singer doing a deal with the devil in Spain.

Cost Adele's soul.

5th March

Just back from the vets.

He was telling me about how he was singing a Righteous Brothers song whilst he cleaned in between a cat's teeth.

The cat thought it was very funny.

I said, "You flossed that laughing feline?" but he said it was 'Unchained Melody'.

6th March

Was supposed to be going to see The Rolling Stones later.

They had to postpone the gig after their guitarist found an actual parasitic arachnid in his ear.

Which was a real tick in the Keith.

7th March

Exciting news!

My new invention works! It can read the minds of high-ranking army officers.

I won't go into the details, but you get the General idea.

8th March

Just back from the pub.

I only went for 'Naked Happy Hour'.

But I stayed until clothing time.

9th March

I've spent all day setting up a Beatles pun contest.

I'm really hoping I can persuade Paul McCartney to HeyJudicate.

10th March

Felt a bit odd at breakfast this morning.

I said to my wife, "I don't know what you've been putting in my oatmeal but it makes me feel kind of trippy and recently it's been getting worse."

She said, "Higher porridge highs?"

Reader, I forgave her.

11th March

Was just trying to write a multilingual numbers joke, but I don't know if it's worth it.

In my experience they've usually cinq without a tres.

12th March

Mr. Willis from Die Hard was in my local bakery this morning!

He was whistling an Elvis song* and putting profiteroles and éclairs on some scales.

*Bruce weighed chouxs

13th March

I'm TERRIBLE at my new job selling plastic canopies!

Even so there's some great perks.

My boss has told me I'm getting a vinyl awning tomorrow!

14th March

Kids!!!

Even though I pay for satellite TV, my daughter insists on only watching Freeview.

I've been putting up with it for far too long.

Well no more, Miss, tonight Sky!

15th March

Went for a jog this morning.

I noticed that an old, run-down building nearby has been renovated so it can be used to host the lavish launch party for a new aftershave.

I suppose that's gent whiff occasion for you.

16th March

We've just got a new pet snake. It's tiny!

It likes to curl up in my baby daughter's glove. You can hear it sometimes, but not always.

It's a little mitten hiss.

17th March

Got a phone call earlier.

I've been asked to direct a sea snail theatre group's production of a Shakespeare tragedy.

I'm steering whelk Lear!

18th March

A very sad day. It was the funeral and cremation of my pet gibbon this afternoon.

They said I might be the greatest pastry chef in the world at the wake, as I'd made a delicious smoky-tasting open tart.

But it was just ape ash in the flan

19th March

Our new baby goat came home with us today.

I'm going to call him 'Humphrey Bogart', because he has a lopsided head.

Ears looking askew, kid!

20th March

I don't know much about Greek mythology (it's my Achilles ankle), but I've been reading up on it this morning.

I reckon Perseus killing Medusa was a gorgon conclusion.

21st March

A long-necked wading bird keeps nesting in my little remote controlled aircraft.

I was a bit annoyed at first, but I've started to bond with it and I quite like it now.

My wife thinks I might be suffering with stork homes in drone.

22nd March

I overheard a policeman talking to a holy woman earlier. I've represented the scene as faithfully as I can below:

> I'D LIKE TO ADVISE YOU OF THE MISAPPROPRIATION OF A MOTHER SUPERIOR
>
> I NEED THAT IN SIMPLER LANGUAGE PLEASE. NO OFFENCE.
>
> NUN TAKEN.

@pauleggleston

23rd March

Just turned on the TV and saw Tom Jones singing 'The Green, Green Grass of Home'.

I thought I'd check what was on the other side and he was singing 'The Greener, Greener Grass of Home'.

24th March

Going through some old holiday photos today.

I was reminiscing about when I had to return a copy of '1984' to a library in Greece, and they were all like:

Orwell, Orwell, Orwell uh huh,
Eighty-Four, Eighty-Four,
Did you get very far?
Eighty-Four, Eighty-Four,
Like with dystopia?'

Wait no, it was a library in GREASE.

25th March

So annoying!

My son has just put a James Bond DVD on the gaudy worktop where we always put our takeaway food deliveries - I'd only just polished it, and it's still damp.

On our mad 'Just Eats' sleek wet surface.

26th March

Film night tonight.

Just watched 'Jurassic Park' and I don't understand why the theme song wasn't 'Lab Amber'.

27th March

Just back from the bakery. It has quite the history, apparently!

They were telling me about when Oscar Wilde called in on his way to purchase a little funereal car for his deceased lamp-dwelling spirit.

He had muffin; chewed éclair; bought his genie hearse.

28th March

Just been on the internet, and found out that apparently in the next series of 'Line Of Duty', suspicions of police interference in events at Mount Vesuvius in 79AD lead to a new job for AE-12 - The Antique Eruption Unit.

29th March

I was waiting to buy a sandwich toaster earlier, when I saw the greatest martial artist ever to come out of Athens walk past.

I didn't know whether to go and get his autograph, or proceed with my purchase.

I was caught between the Breville and the Greek Bruce Lee.

30th March

The local art gallery has promised me that they'll invest more in their curation after they got an Impressionist painting mixed up with a Precisionist work.

Sounds promising, but I think it's about time they put their Monet where Demuth is.

31st March

Found out today that apparently the best way to ask a guy to marry you is to find a rural vista and wear a fluffy Japanese robe.

Make kimono furry, country views.

APRIL

BREAKING NEWS...
THE EASTER BUNNY HAS
BEEN STRUCK DOWN WITH...
   PICK + MIXOMATOSIS

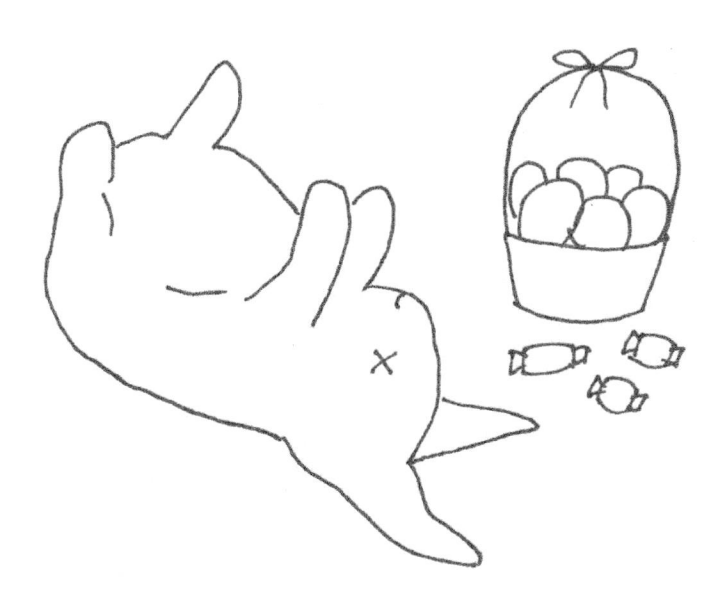

1st April

> My wife is insisting on driving me to a restaurant to buy me a puréed fruit dessert of my choice.
>
> She must take me for some kind of fool...

2nd April

> Spent most of today trying to think of an anagram of 'naive twosome'.
>
> Not a wise move...

3rd April

> Was just fondly reminiscing* about when I had those bath-sheets with the Viking cats on, and thought they were elegantly fashionable.
>
> *Feline Norse towel chic.

4th April

Lionel Richie was supposed to be painting my portrait today, but it looked suspiciously like a piece of fan art depicting Mark Hamill's character in Star Wars playing the Norse God of Thunder in Marvel's eponymous film.

I was like, "Hello? Is it me or Luke in Thor?"

5th April

Was just reading about how one of the Norman Kings liked to pull flamboyant stunts on his bike whilst impersonating a mallard.

He was wheelie ham, duck honkerer.

6th April

My wife wanted to try to win some underwear in a 60s dance competition this evening

I said not to be so daft...

But then she went and got her knickers in a Twist.

7th April

Calling around all the local monasteries today to ask if they might be interested in me giving mild electric shocks to the monks, to improve their vocal performance.

Just on the off chants.

8th April

Just about to head out for a ramble.

I used to plaster myself with animal fat before I went for a long walk, but I can't be bothered any more.

It's too much hike lard work.

9th April

My halo manufacturing business is still doing ok!

I was a bit worried about the heavy cost of materials, but it turns out that's balanced out by the light overheads.

10th April

I'm sure the woman at the pet shop fancies me.

I was there earlier - I saw her coming back from feeding the creatures in the aquatic section and she made very flirty eye-contact.

Or maybe that's just fish-full winking?

11th April

Our local priest died in a skydiving accident recently.

The church owl wanted to say a few words today at the funeral, but insisted someone else spoke first.

Unfortunately the parish hoot didn't open.

12th April

My wife and I should have been going to France for Easter but we decided against it as we always end up arguing about whether either of us deserves an egg.

We have an earn an oeuf relationship.

13th April

A group of crows was booked in for my mindfulness class tomorrow, but they just had to cancel.

Apparently they can't come because they've been arrested for pre-meditated murder.

14th April

Went out for dinner with my wife this evening.

It was very quiet, then the waiter came to the table and said, "Cheese board?"

So I said, "Look, I'm trying my best mate. You try saying something interesting after twenty years of marriage."

15th April

Just got another mysterious call from the local football team's coach.

I think my wife might have been secretly taking goalkeeping lessons.

I certainly wouldn't put it past her.

16th April

My daughter just said, "I'm so sick of being single!"

So I said, "Can't you woo someone?"

She said, "Woo who?"

So that's great that she's feeling better already!

17th April

Hosting the Archaeology Oscars this evening!

I'm just about to give out the award for the best excavation of a patella belonging one of William the Conqueror's knights.

And the Norman knees are...

18th April

Stopped to get a hotdog from a roadside café today, on my way to recover a van that had broken down, and take it to a museum. It contained the skeleton of a stallion that belonged to Joan of Arc.

I was telling the hotdog guy about it, and he said, "Tow martyr's horse?"

So I said, "Yes, and mustard please."

19th April

>Kids!!!

>Honestly, if you leave your balaclava outside all night, then get a cold face because it's wet around the edge of the bit you look through then I'm sorry...

>But eye-hole dew responsible!

20th April

>Reading a FABULOUS book about the invention of the spring.

>It's a classic story of when boing meets curl.

21st April

>Just got my pay-slip through.

>When I looked in the envelope there was a fountain pen refill and someone's toupee in there too. I was absolutely livid.

>Ink and hair sent with wage.

22nd April

Off to see The Verve play a gig at our dilapidated village hall this evening.

It will have to be an acoustic set though, because the plugs don't work.

23rd April

Started a new job today, giving out glazed biscuits in the shapes of letters of the alphabet.

"Can I offer you a frosted 'B'?" I said to one man.

"No, I'm fine thank you!" came the reply.

"Ok. Have a nice day!" I said.

But then he said, "No, I said I'm fine THANK YOU!"

24th April

Bumped into Mick Jagger earlier. What a great guy!

I asked him whether, reflecting on his career, his memories are more happy, or melancholy. He says seven tenths of his memories are happy.

Then he's tried, and he's tried, but he can't get no saddest fraction.

25th April

Just found out that the landlord at my local pub nicked the brewery inspector's diary.

He got 12 months behind bars.

26th April

That Knight Rider bloke is always in my local Indian restaurant, and he's in here now.

Every time he complains that his flatbread's too hot and every time he gets a friend to fan it with a children's book*.

*The crony cools Hoff naan here.

27th April

Just seen Andrew Lloyd Webber.

He was wafting air at an overheating cat that was covered in dirt, backstage at one of his shows*.

*Fanned a muddy hot purrer.

28th April

John Travolta has FINALLY sent through that gadget that applies peroxide to large waterbirds

Why this goose-bleaching machine is automatic...

It's systematic...

It's hyyyyyyydromatic...

Why it's geese whitening!!!

29th April

So proud of myself right now. It was the first day of my levitation lessons today.

I went straight to the top of the class!

30th April

SCANDAL!

The local French-owned creamery is having a light meal tonight to mark the decommissioning of their oldest butter-making machine.

It's meant to be TOP SECRET, but a guy who works there told me!

That's a dairy leaked churn 'adieu' tea.

MAY

MY WIFE AND I CAN'T AGREE ON APPROPRIATE GARDENING FOOTWEAR. BUT SHE'S DIGGING IN HER HEELS...

@pauleggleston

1st May

> FINALLY!
>
> After years of trying, I've successfully cross-bred a crocodile with a homing pigeon.
>
> Though I expect that'll come back to bite me.

2nd May

> Following yesterday's achievement...
>
> I took my genetic engineering exam recently, and it was results day today.
>
> I passed with flying koalas!

3rd May

> Just worn out *another* cheese-shredding utensil, so I'm building a new, very hard-wearing one into my kitchen...
>
> Because I'm really integrating.

4th May

Written a poem for Star Wars Day:

Once pined a Jedi named Yoda,
That inclined his way of speaking,
To titter his friends,
Which bitter made him,
Plus his limericks rhymed none of.

5th May

Went for an interview today.

The bloke asked me to scream, then hit him, sneeze, and finally put on a nightdress.

Which seemed a bit weird but at least I knew it was a fair process, as they are an 'eek!', 'wallop!', 'achoo!', nighties employer.

6th May

I'm SO angry right now. A quartet of small burrowing mammals has infiltrated my singing group, in disguise.

I'm going to identify them today by giving everyone a diuretic that is only effective for those creatures, and see who runs to the toilet.

I'm initiating a four mole in choir wee.

7th May

It's a TERRIBLE idea that they're trying to get the original Indiana Jones back for a new film where he's searching for an ancient list of ingredients.

I mean, it's a recipe Ford is after...

8th May

Just looked out of my window and saw this herd of elements!

A HERD OF ELEMENTS

@pauleggleston

9th May

Took one of the cats to the vet today as she is excessively fluffy just under her mouth.

They think it's because she loves to drink extra fur chin olive oil.

10th May

Saw on the news that Elton John has very generously paid for his local church to import two toilets from Belgrade to accommodate the priest's assistant, who has an unusually large bottom.

And I guess that's wide acolyte's Serb loos.

11th May

SO EXCITED to reveal today that I've managed to cross a monkey with an ape, and I've trained it to always come back to me.

I call it a Baboomerangutan.

12th May

Went to see a so-called 'Spice Girls tribute act' this evening.

There was no Ginger, Baby or Posh, but there were two Sporty Spices and two Scary Spices.

I wasn't happy, so I decided to register a four Mel complaint.

13ᵗʰ May

>Today I've been trying to teach a goose to shout 'NO!' in German.
>
>It was a real struggle, but he finally got it just now.
>
>He looks so pleased with himself.
>
>He's honked loud 'NEIN!'

14ᵗʰ May

>Just had another one of those nuisance phone calls.
>
>He's still going on about his weighty block of soft French cheese.
>
>It's the heavy brie thing again.

15ᵗʰ May

>I was supposed to be making a little frame for smoking fish on today - it didn't work out perfectly.
>
>But at least I've haddock rack.

16th May

> Just heard that the local zoo wants to call Leo the lion 'Kojak' because all his hair fell out.
>
> I know the zookeeper there, but he shall rename maneless.

17th May

> Been sorting out my music collection today
>
> I still haven't found my 'I Still Haven't Found What I'm Looking For' CD.
>
> Oh wait, there it is, under my 'Whoomp! (There It Is)' CD.

18th May

> I need to show the number 7 in Roman numerals.
>
> I've already written a V, which is something I want two capital I's on.

19th May

> I KEEP telling my wife I don't want my mattress suspended vertically outside the house, but she won't listen.
>
> It's like I'm hanging my bed against a brick wall.

20th May

Just watched a new documentary* exploring the ethics of an increasing number of mallards drinking Bombay Sapphire and Gordon's.

People are saying it isn't balanced, but I'm very impressed with its pro duck gin values.

*duckumentary

21st May

Jury service today.

The judge took an instant dislike to the bloke next to me, who was originally from Paris, because his expensive sandwich fell apart.

He reminded me of that Jim Carrey character.

Hates French juror, Pret defective.

22nd May

Jury service again!

The accused claimed that he couldn't have committed the crime because he hadn't had anything to eat on the evening in question.

So we found the defendant got nil tea.

23rd May

Sad news.

I failed my piccolo exam.

My tutor has said he'll only let me take it again after I've put some WD40 on all the keys and levers, so I suppose I'll have to do that.

Resit stance is flute oil.

24th May

I just saw an Australian lady on the TV singing:

'I'm spinning around,
Move out of my way,
If you don't move out of my way I shall become more
powerful than you can possibly imagine.'

I think it was Obi-Wan Minoguey.

25th May

Good news / bad news today!

I'm allowed to travel by air again!

But now I'm stuck in a hotel lobby.

Out of the flying ban, into the foyer...

26th May

>It shakes her nerves and it rattles her brain.

>Too much Swiss cheese drives my nan insane.

>She flipped a stall at the village hall.

>Goodness gracious, fête brawls of Gruyere!

27th May

>Yuck.

>The committee for the Star Trek convention I just attended, in the largest town in Angus, was so big and unwieldy that they missed the important details, like ensuring adequate toilet facilities for the cosplayers.

>Too many Kirks soiled Arbroath.

28th May

>Kermit and Miss Piggy's wedding was an odd occasion.

>He was using a walking frame, whilst she wore a dickie bow. But I'm so pleased I was invited.

>It was a one-zimmer-wife-tie muppet unity.

29th May

Just reading a book about a vampire.

He just said, "I vant to suck your blood! But first look at that cute baby sheep! I simply must pet it!"

It's Lamb Stroker's Dracula

30th May

Someone stopped me in the street earlier and asked where I learned to walk like I do.

"On parade in western Canada," I said.

"Vancouvery march!" came the reply.

So I told her she was very welcome.

31st May

Saw a military recruitment video showing the Terminator fixing a TV receiver on a castle tower.

It was so good that I've decided to join the turret aerial Arnie.

JUNE

I WENT INTO THE SHOP AT WIMBLEDON, SHOWED THEM MY RECEIPT, AND SAID "I'D LIKE TO RETURN THESE, PLEASE."

THEY SAID "WELL, YOU'LL JUST HAVE TO TAKE LESSONS LIKE EVERYONE ELSE, SIR!"

@pauleggleston

1st June

> Just woke up from a crazy dream!!
>
> I dreamt that I weighed less than a thousandth of a gram!
>
> I was, like, 0mg!!!

2nd June

> Spoke to a friend who is a judge earlier.
>
> Apparently you won't go to prison for punching a tortilla.
>
> But you might get a wrap on the knuckles.

3rd June

> I have long suspected that my pet parrot's wavy hairstyle isn't natural, so I got up at the crack of dawn today and sure enough found him treating it with chemicals.
>
> The curly bird thatch is a perm.

4th June

Trying to get on the internet for some medical advice, as I've sprouted tropical bird feathers under my chin.

But I'm struggling toucan-necked.

5th June

Went to the doctors because my leg hurt.

I said I thought it was my cruise-ship ligament.

He laughed and said I meant 'cruciate'.

But I had the last laugh because he was the one who got deafened by the foghorn in my knee.

6th June

Just saw a picture of Jay Kay lying on the bottom of a bunk bed.

That bloke out of Ultravox was on the top bunk, reading him a Pierre Boulle novel.

It was Midge over Jamiroquai.

7th June

Very frustrating train journey today.

I doubt I'll get anywhere by emailing the train company about the lack of conductors.

But I'll send it re: guardless.

8th June

I've been sampling liquidised Teletubby today.

The nicest smelling one was the Po puree.

9th June

Just been telling my friend how I can't eat anything without immediately getting food in my beard.

Not in person though, we were online*.

*Instant messy chin.

10th June

I'm now offering light afternoon meals in a two-wheeled horse-drawn vehicle.

But I'll have to pick people up from their houses.

Because apparently chariot tea begins at home.

11th June

My ex-wife wants us to go to marriage guidance counselling because of my nautical obsession, but I've remarried already.

So obviously that ship has sailed!

12th June

My neighbour passed away recently and I've just found out that he bequeathed everything to a crack in the Earth's crust.

Lovely man, he was.

Always generous to a fault.

13th June

Spent today sticking stuff together with glue.

No, wait...

Actually, I spent the day singing a rendition of 'Hallelujah' that was *very* faithful to the original.

Honestly, sometimes I don't know whether I'm gumming or Cohen.

14th June

Just been fired for telling everyone in the office that I double in size when there's a full moon.

Apparently that's technically growth myth conduct.

15th June

On this day in 1215 the Magna Carta was signed.

But what no one ever talks about was that there was a mistake on the document because it said 'Magma Carta', so King John screamed and jumped on his throne.

They'd just invented the game 'The Flaw is Lava'.

16th June

Help!!

I've rescued a tiny Prunus Avium that was growing in my fruit pie and I don't know what to do with it.

It's completely untarted cherry tree.

17th June

My friend is dating a Detective Inspector, who is currently working undercover in a butcher's.

He sounds a bit dull but apparently there's more to him than meats DI.

18th June

Called a sanctuary for semi-aquatic mammals in Tel Aviv this morning.

The receptionist said, "Hello, Israeli Otter Home?"

I said, "No, I don't even live with Ray Liotta. Anyway I called you."

19th June

Applied for a job with a travel agent today. They specialise in Australian wildlife holidays and want someone with experience.

I'm a bit worried that I lack the relevant koala vacations.

20th June

Saw a man holding an electric revolving door for a lady today, in the middle of a powercut.

And they said that swivelry was dead!

21st June

Heard the tabby that lives in the toilet at my kids' nursery today. I swear it sounded like it was singing 'Against All Odds'

(Daycare loo cat meow...)

22nd June

I'm cosplaying as Dick Dastardly later, and I'm borrowing a dog to take with me.

It doesn't look EXACTLY right, but it is a proxy Muttley.

23rd June

We went out for a meal this evening and had a terrible time. I asked to speak to the manager but he was busy and sent a tender beef fillet to resolve the complaint. I found that unacceptable.

I wanted to talk to the boss, not one of his mignons.

24th June

Someone keeps phoning up pretending to be my grandmother.

It's a prank, I don't know what else to call it.

My wife suggested 'Shenanigan', so she's now my number one suspect.

25th June

Tough day today.

Ever since we got that set of Chinese frying pans, engraved with 'husband' and 'wife', our relationship has been on the woks.

26th June

I wanted a roast dinner earlier, but I was in a hurry so I asked the bloke at the pub, "Is your carvery fast?"

He said he'd never had cause to go much over 70 in it.

27th June

My ox got poisoned earlier, and the evidence (that it's because someone's pen leaked onto its drinking receptacle) is pretty watertight.

Ink on trough hurt a bull, in fact.

28th June

Lesson learned today.

Never EVER buy an office chair off a weatherman. I picked mine up earlier.

It's only ever had four casters on it.

29th June

Had to leave a WhatsApp group just now, because there was a discussion about the best synonym for a tea strainer.

I just couldn't deal with all the 'a brew sieve' messages.

30th June

This week I've received a nasty letter each day, each signed by a different sausagey-sounding cleric. And they're getting more and more horrible.

Today's was by Father Wurst.

JULY

MY BEACH BBQ WAS A SHORE-FIRE-SUCCESS
@paulegglestan

1st July

Just having a coffee with a woman who was David Bowie's Head of Security at his concerts, when she was a very young mother.

'This is crowd control teenager mom...'

2nd July

Washed my Shakespeare doll earlier, and couldn't work out how to dry it on the washing line.

I asked my wife and she said, "Peg your bard on!"

So I asked her again.

3rd July

My lovely pet stag has started making some weird sheep noises, but I can't make it stay in one place so I can get a video of it.

Be still my bleating hart!

4th July

I know a LOT about motor vehicles.

I was locked in the trunk of a French car this morning, and was still able to identify how powerful the engine was.

I always think if you can't do that then you simply don't know voiture torque in a boot.

5th July

Saw a little outbuilding earlier with a sign that said

'ONTO LEGS'

I was a bit confused until I realised it was actually the

'GENTS LOO'

But it was out of order.

6th July

Ever since I was bitten by that radioactive owl the other day, I've been making all my wife's decisions for her.

I've been given power of a tawny.

I AM "OWL MAN", AND MY SUPER ABILITY IS MAKING YOUR DECISIONS FOR YOU!

POWER OF A TAWNY

7th July

My kids want to tattoo each other with the image of an emaciated-looking George VI. It's the latest trend.

Are youth inking wartime thin king?

8th July

We had to evacuate the office at work today, to the tune of 'Boogie Wonderland'.

Someone had set off the Earth, Wind & Fire alarm.

9th July

Popped into the Angora Goat Fabric Emporium this afternoon and batted my eyelashes at the staff.

Because apparently fluttery gets you mohair.

10th July

I recently bought Boy George's chameleon off him but it's been a bit stressed.

It's only calmed down today after I installed a flap for it, so it could come and go.

11th July

Once again my wife has left so little petrol in the car that I can only get as far as the pub.

It's enough to drive me to drink.

But obviously not back again. DON'T DRINK & DRIVE, KIDS!!!

12th July

Sometimes I feel like I can't do anything right.

My wife asked me to go to the garden centre so I'm there now and she's just staring at me out of the kitchen window.

13th July

Apparently there's increasing incidents of people leaving their fridge open *just* long enough for a small songbird to get in, then unwittingly trapping it inside.

WON'T SOMEBODY THINK OF THE CHILLED WREN??

14th July

ANOTHER job interview today.

I spoke about the time I was put in charge of the sample pots of silvery emulsion at the paint factory, and my boss offered me a congratulatory polo.

Because THAT was my grey tester chief mint.

15th July

Saw a friend today, the one who talks complete rubbish.

He reckons he got a tattoo of a sad pigeon on his shin the other day, but that's just a low dove below knee.

16th July

Popped to the bank earlier.

A gun-wielding jelly came in and stole a large amount of cash.

According to the police, it's just the latest in a series of armed wobblies.

17th July

Supposed to be going to visit my mate in hospital today.

He tripped over the teepee he used to run his business from, but I still don't know the ex tent-office injuries.

18th July

Meeting up with my brother and sister this evening and I'm already feeling competitive.

I suspect we'll all need to go to the loo immediately upon seeing each other due to the intense sibling arrival wee.

19th July

Did a presentation at work today.

It went pretty well! As usual I ended by sticking a post-it on the ceiling which said 'Kiitos ja näkemiin'.

Always Finnish on a high note.

20th July

Just watching a history programme.

Apparently in Turkey it was customary to set fire to piles of Marshall Mathers memorabilia during the time of the hot Eminem pyre.

21st July

Thinking of setting up a cattery business, just so I can establish a three-stage staff disciplinary procedure, which will be:

    1) Informal furball warning
    2) Final kitten warning
    3) Purrmination of contract

22nd July

Getting lots of complaints at the moment about my latest joke, about involuntary spasms of the diaphragm, but I've heard most of the complainants making jokes about involuntary spasms of the diaphragm themselves!

Well I'm sorry, but that just makes them terrible hiccup wits.

23rd July

My pet snail seems a bit down today, and I'm not sure why.

As a snail owner, I'm aware that apparently they are sensitive to a particular word meaning 'understood' because it has a heteronym that is insulting to those of them with oversized shells.

But I've never fathomed which word that is.

24ᵗʰ July

Got paid a pittance today, so I angrily deposited the money at the bank, slamming it down on the counter with my fist - the one with all the tattoos on it.

Ink hand descent with wage.

25ᵗʰ July

I took ages slicing up a pungent vegetable this evening, which created totally unbearable suspense.

But it was completely onion tension hell.

26ᵗʰ July

Was in a bar earlier

A robot walked in.

The barman said 'wired oblong face?'

27ᵗʰ July

ANOTHER one of our Spanish neighbours has created an Egyptian Pharaoh themed garden.

Honestly, they're like buses.

You can wait for AGES... and then Tutankhamun lawn at Juan's.

28th July

Wanted to buy an ice cream today, but our local seller has managed to get himself arrested!

I don't know what he did, but it must have been bad because apparently he's been put into solid dairy confinement.

29th July

Heard a lady chicken being candid about her achievement in higher education earlier, so naturally I ate a polo.

I always do in that situation, and I always will.

It's an open hen did degree mint.

30th July

The ruffians up the road have been picking on eggs from the north of France again.

"Come and have a go if you think you're Ardennes oeuf!" they keep shouting.

31st July

I've just invented a toilet that tells you how many times you've been for a wee when you flush it.

It's probably my greatest achievement.

My pee history cisterns.

AUGUST

I GOT THIS POSTCARD FROM A FRIEND. THIS IS THE BESTSELLING DESIGN IN THE ITALIAN CAPITAL APPARENTLY. VENN IN ROME !!!

Visit...
ROME

@pauleggleston

1st August

> Bought a smart toaster today, and I've just managed to connect it to the internet!
>
> It's pretty cool, but I'm getting a bit fed up of all the pop-up notifications.

2nd August

> I've been invited to a fancy dress party this evening - the theme is 'abstract ethical concepts'.
>
> I'd rather stay at home, but I'm going to go, as a matter of principle.

3rd August

> Had to call the RSPCA today, because there was a polecat clinging to our ceiling fan.
>
> I don't think they believed me.
>
> But they eventually had to take my whirred ferret.

4th August

Went round to Tina Turner's for a cuppa this afternoon, but unfortunately I broke her sofa.

The pressure exerted by my bottom was over the butt-push settee limit.

5th August

Chatting to my judge friend again this morning. I asked what the best style of boot to wear is, in his line of work.

Apparently it's THIGH LENGTH IN COURT.

6th August

MIGHT have bought some novelty rabbit slippers online last night when I was drunk. My wife's not sure if I did or not.

But she's giving me the bunny feet order doubt.

7th August

My wife keeps threatening to leave, citing my irrational suspicion that she's keeping a secret stash of perfect condition comics featuring the frog from the Muppets.

I think she might have Kermit: mint issues.

8th August

EMBARRASSING!!

Had to take responsibility for a particularly loud guff in the supermarket earlier.

It takes bravery to own up to flatulence.

It's certainly not for the ain't farted.

9th August

Just read that apparently 'Like a Virgin' has only just been translated into the national language of the Netherlands.

Dutch for the very first time!

10th August

Bumped into my daughter and her boyfriend at the convenience store earlier.

They were sitting in the corner wearing pointed hats.

They're in a Londis dunce relationship.

11th August

Just woke up from a dream that I was a zombie, listening to Gloria Gaynor!

At first I was decayed, I was putrefied!

Kept thinking I could never live without formaldehyde...

12th August

Saw one of my garden ornaments bestow a knighthood on a secret agent a little while ago.

He was wearing gloves, and Alice Cooper was playing in the background*.

*Gnome wore mitts to knight spy.

13th August

My wife can keep criticising a piece of material sewn into a garment to strengthen or enlarge a part of it as much as she wants.

But I don't wish to diss gusset.

14th August

I've been invited to an Anaesthetists' Ball, but I've been told to bring lipstick and mascara with me.

I think they're only asking me to make up the numbers.

15th August

Football Association – check!

Farmer's Almanac – check!

Family Allowance – check!

Flight Attendant – check!

Fibonacci Association – check!

(Sorry, it's just FAs I'm going through...)

16th August

This bloke came up to me today and said, "Slightly regretted."

I thought 'that's a bit rued.'

17th August

My wife threatened to leave me today because of my insistence on cataloguing my bicycle collection using French numbers.

But then I went out and bought my eleventh, and she decided to let bike onze be bike onze.

18th August

Went on the local Facebook group today, to ask what I should do if I find an insect with its antennae on fire.

Just thought I'd put out the feelers.

19th August

Got fired from Argos today after designing a brochure containing only clothes horses.

It was a catalogue of airers.

20th August

Dreamt that the Rolling Stones singer was planning a series of bank safe heists, either using a prosthetic face or dressed as a holy woman. But whilst he's generally competent, he didn't think he'd be skilled enough to pull it off.

It was a case of Jagger vault raids, masked or a nun.

21ˢᵗ August

Got a quote for putting my German vacuum cleaner into storage today but it's too expensive.

And they're not giving me any room for mein hoover.

22ⁿᵈ August

Just saw on the news that a number of fashionable, upper class, female sheep have been spotted in London.

It must be a Sloane Ewes day...

23ʳᵈ August

Met a very odd chap today who said he likes starting fires by rubbing two pens together.

I think he might be a biromaniac.

24th August

In the supermarket earlier.

A security guard came up and said, "Can I ask how long you're planning on walking around the store with a frozen chicken down each trouser leg?"

I said, "Sure!"

So he put a frozen chicken down each trouser leg and asked, "How long are you planning on walking around the store?"

25th August

Stopped to help Barbie's boyfriend earlier as his car had broken down.

He called the recovery service but they would only offer to send a medieval joker to haul him home.

Which seemed like it was just a tow Ken jester.

26th August

Really want someone to help me out with finding an anagram of 'bun looter'.

But only if it's no trouble...

27th August

I just found out that the patron saint of not being in love is St Francis of 10cc.

> THE PATRON SAINT OF NOT BEING IN LOVE IS ST. FRANCIS OF 10cc
> @pauleggleston

28th August

I've been using my wife's mascara wand to scratch in between my shoulder blades today.

It's resulted in a backlash.

29th August

Ordered some Elvis memorabilia that should have come today.

I'm still waiting for it though because it's been held up in the depot.

In the depoooot.

(I'm hoping they don't Return to Sender)

30th August

The kitten has gone a bit strange today.

Probably shouldn't have showed it that Diabolist marketing video.

But I was just playing devil's ad for cat.

31st August

Plácido Domingo borrowed my arrow container today.

I'm not sure exactly how much its worth – maybe around £9.99 - but it's definitely a quiver lent to a tenor.

SEPTEMBER

"I thought it would be funny to send my daughter back to school dressed as a citrus fruit, to take her mind off her upcoming tests."

"SATS humour?"

"No, a clementine"

@pauleggleston

1st September

>My daughter just told me that I look like the back of a boat.

>I must have had my stern face on.

2nd September

>Went to the doctors today because I keep thinking I'm a musical instrument.

>I can't remember what he said, but I did make lots of notes.

3rd September

>I'm injecting male walrus hormones so I get the body one of my favourite action movie stars.

>It's Seal testosterone.

>Or I'll settle for Arnold Schwarzenegger.

4th September

My wife said we needed a chat earlier.

But she knows I'm allergic and I didn't want to spend ALL of our French holiday in the pet shop.

5th September

Went for a nice little walk on our break in France.

At first my wife didn't like the small stream we saw because she objected to the way it intersected with another stream, but as we walked along she grew quite fond of it.

So you should never judge a brook by its carrefour.

6th September

Feeling a bit sad today.

Ever since I found out that I'm genetically predisposed to being the same height as a tall flightless long-necked bird, I've been ostrich-sized from my family.

7th September

From today I've decided to stop driving along with my bum out of the window, beeping my horn.

I'm worried that I might end up in a mysterious accident due to the curse of 'Tooting Car Moon'.

8th September

Was overcharged for a jelly this morning.

Daylight wobbly.

9th September

Just watching a science program.

Some scientists come out with some really obvious stuff.

I mean, I could have told them that a big bang can make a ewe nervous.

10th September

Just found an ancient packet of long grain in my cupboard and I'm very scared of it.

I'm worried it might be THE ANTIQUE RICE...

11th September

Took a leather cash and card holder with me on a long walk today.

I didn't know how long it would last, but it turned out to be very hike wallety.

12th September

I recently cross bred a bull with a chameleon on the cheap, but I'm regretting it now.

I wasn't prepared for all the hidden charges.

13th September

Saw some friends this afternoon.

I told them that their six-month old baby was 'age a half', but they said he just has a long neck.

14th September

Went to a pet shop today to buy a mole on credit but they wouldn't let me.

I even offered them a VERY svelte honey-making insect as collateral. But it was still a no.

Neither a burrower nor a slender bee.

15th September

Have recently taken up amateur dramatics.

Today I asked the director to rate my ability to take direction and he just said 'below average'.

So I bellowed 'AVERAGE!!!'

16th September

After this evening I would not recommend contacting a dead homing pigeon with an Ouija board.

It will just end up coming back to haunt you.

17th September

Really enjoying my new job looking after plant pots and hanging baskets for celebrities.

It means that I tend to shrub holders with the rich and famous.

18th September

Just invented a loaf of bread that says 'Good Morning!' in German.

I've also invented one that just says 'Morning!' in German, that's the guten-free version.

19th September

I'm behind with the washing, so a bit embarrassed to be wearing my emergency Ricky Martin 'Livin' la Vida Loca' t-shirt today.

But on the upside, it's inside-out.

20th September

Went to marriage guidance counselling today.

My wife complained that I misunderstand everything.

The counsellor asked me what she means.

So I told her it's a feminine pronoun.

21st September

Going to have to read my kids the riot act this evening.

They're developing an interest in historic British legislation, and it seems to get them off to sleep.

22nd September

Back at the doctors today because I keep thinking I'm going to float away.

She asked how that makes me feel, and I said, "Gloomy... Down..."

So she did.

Ruined the chair.

23rd September

Successfully applied a dressing to a laceration on my tortoise today.

That was gauze for shell abrasion!

24th September

Just downloaded a fancy new app that reviews high street clothing stores.

What will they think of Next?

25th September

Written the synopsis for a book entitled 'The Exhumation of Winnie The Pooh' today.

It's just the bear bones at the moment.

26th September

Had to close my hearing aid hire business today.

I got into renter ears.

27th September

Got a brilliant new job pushing a dessert trolley around at the local jazz café.

It's a new dawn
It's a new day
It's a new life
For me...

AND I'M WHEELING PUD..

28th September

What a day!

No one was available to operate on my cow earlier.

I ended up passing out due to lack of ox surgeon.

29th September

Apparently I was talking in my sleep last night.

First I murmured, "I love them scrambled!" but a bit later I shouted, "NO! NOT POACHED!"

I went from one eggs dream to another.

30th September

Saw a poster earlier that announced 'Leann Rimes with special guest'.

But it definitely doesn't.

OCTOBER

YOU'RE IN THE NEWSPAPER TODAY, DAHLING!
VERE? I CAN'T SEE ANYTHING?
Mirror
@pauleggleston

1st October

>Popped into the bank today and said, "I'd like to take some money from my account please."

>The bloke said, "Withdrawal?"

>So I said, "Aaaahd liiiiike to taaaaaake some muuuuuhney from my accouuuuunt puhleeeassse."

2nd October

>Today was going so badly that I tried to cheer everyone up by making a duck sneeze.

>But I was just peppering over the quacks.

3rd October

>Honestly, the state of this country.

>6 out of 8 people don't know a synonym for flooding.

>Or, in other words, freak waters.

4th October

That annoying bloke knocked on the door this morning, asking to come in.

I said, "Sorry, I need to pop out. My uncle's poorly wife needs something to store her sausages in so I'm taking her this flimsy bowl."

So he said, "Weak aunt keep meat in light dish?"

But he's the one who keeps turning up unannounced...

5th October

Oh my goodness, I found a rare early draft of 'Gone with the Wind' in a second-hand book shop today!

It's pretty much the same, except at the end Scarlett expresses a desire to observe a Madagascan primate on a stag's back, from the side; then post a Krispy Kreme animation on social media; and finally eat some Dutch cheese.

Of course this prompts Rhett's famous line, "Flank lemur deer-ride; donut gif; Edam

6th October

Written a script for a low-budget version of The Tempest.

It's just a draught at the moment.

7th October

Just bet a hyena £1000 that he couldn't swim across a river.

Now he's laughing all the way to the bank.

8th October

Went into a car showroom today and said, "I want a car with an illuminated horn." The bloke said, "Beeper light?"

So I said, "PLEASE may I have a car with an illuminated horn."

9th October

My wife just asked when I'd be de-scaling the kettle.

But I've only just reached its summit and the views of the kitchen are breathtaking.

10th October

Played Monopoly with my wife this evening, but it wasn't going well for her.

So she tipped a whole bottle of 'citrus fresh' toilet cleaner over the instructions.

Which was a fragrant bleach of the rules.

11th October

My inkjet keeps stopping for long pauses between little bits of activity, which is quite annoying.

I wish I'd never called it 'Harold Printer'.

12th October

Was in a restaurant earlier and said, "You've given me three whole carrots, but I'd like them cubed."

So the waiter apologised and returned with 27 whole carrots.

13th October

My son met a girl at 'Camouflage Club' recently. It's going pretty well.

They've been not seeing each other for a couple of months now.

14th October

Apparently on this day in 1066 King Harold sat on seven bees and a wasp.

He ended up with a butthole of eight stings.

15th October

Everyone keeps saying that I need to stop thinking I'm a brush.

I have to be honest, that really makes me bristle.

16th October

Just been looking into buying a new drill.

I honestly think they're the best tools in the hole whirled.

17th October

My wife's getting pretty angry that I always take my novelty Old MacDonald biro to bed with me.

I'll be sleeping with one EIEIO-pen tonight.

18th October

Disappointing evening.

My ill-fated plan to count up all the entertaining nightclub bouncers in town this evening was fun doormen tally flawed.

19th October

Was just trying to think of an anagram of 'foolish otters'.

But then I thought 'life's too short'…

20th October

I swear the acorn tree in my garden is possessed by a spirit, which I appreciate sounds very unusual.

It keeps disagreeing with me in French.

Oak haunt rare!

21st October

Been out all day trying to sell a thermos with absolutely no capacity for any liquid.

It's a tankless flask.

22nd October

Just completed my dissertation on patterns in flatulence amongst unmarried men.

I thought it was for an MSc, but it turns out it's a Bachelor farts.

23rd October

Went to the opticians today. I've drawn what happened.

24th October

Saw a pony at the farm that kept closing one of its eyes, so I coaxed it over to my little girl to show her, but it stopped.

So you can lead a horse to daughter, but you can't make it wink.

25th October

My son wanted a proper drum kit for his birthday but I got him a miniature one.

I'm now expecting wee percussions.

26th October

Bought a tartan chameleon today. It was £100.

Which included all the background checks.

27th October

Just read a book about a couple of footballers' wives who developed magical powers.

It was a WAGs to witches story.

28th October

Had a little chat with the Grim Reaper earlier.

Apparently his wife has just left him for a bloke with a pair of small pruning shears.

Which proves once and for all that scythe doesn't matter.

29th October

Taking some friends on my ghost walk tonight.

The forecast is for rain, but I won't let that dampen my spirits.

30th October

Apparently a ghost was seen stealing a towboat from Gdańsk today.

It was a Pole tug heist.

31st October

Someone just knocked on my door and said I had to give them a small branch, or they would twist my nipple. Bloody twig or tweakers.

NOVEMBER

THE INVENTION OF FIREWORKS WAS 'HISSS...' TO 'WHEEEE!' IN THE MAKING...

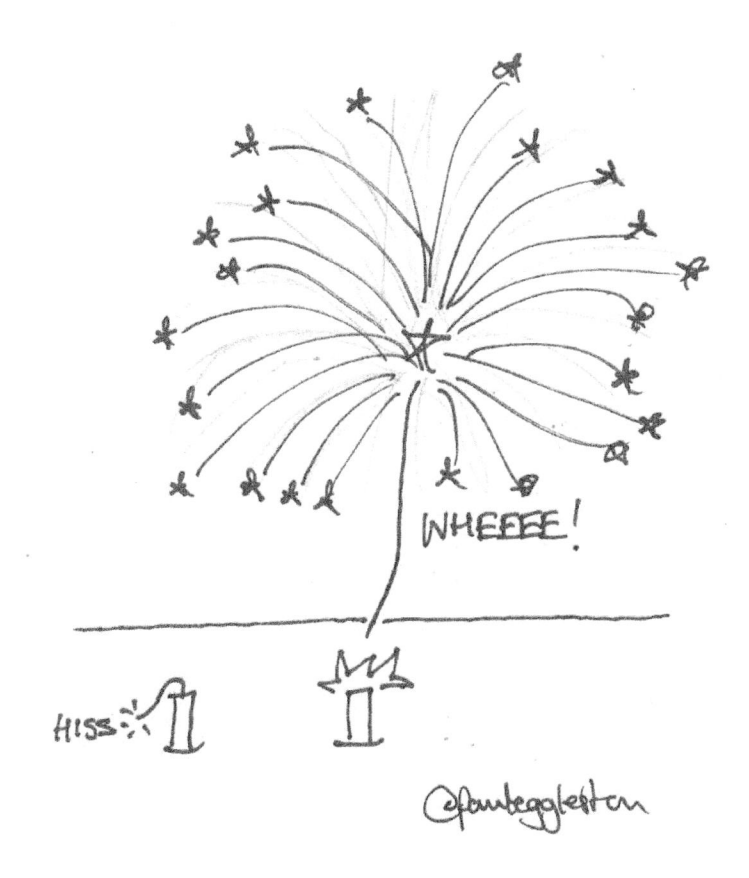

WHEEEE!

HISS

@paulegglestm

1st November

> I HATE EXERCISE.
>
> Ran a marathon today with a dollop of mayonnaise in my beard.
>
> I've just been admitted to hospital with egg sauce chin.

2nd November

> I'm going to think of an anagram of 'that is no delight'.
>
> Even if it's the last thing I do...

3rd November

> Earlier I told my wife she'd never be able to build a large receptacle for storing frozen water.
>
> But ice tank erected.

4th November

I saw an odd magician bring a small chicken back from the dead today.

It was a little ex-hen trick.

5th November

About to set up a stall selling Chinese frying pans in a hotel lobby, though the manager doesn't know it yet...

There's gonna be foyer woks!

6th November

Been trying to think of a term synonymous with boiling an egg.

Maybe I'm not thinking harden oeuf.

7th November

I've decided that when I die, I'd like my ashes scattered in a West African canal.

Waterway Togo...

8th November

Just off to invest some old slivers of wood at the bank.

I've removed all the little nails.

So I can put them in a tacks-free shavings account.

9th November

I stumbled across The Almighty's office today, in a labyrinth of fragrant climbing shrubs.

Turns out God works in wisterias maze.

10th November

On this day in 1871, Henry Morton Stanley found a rock by Lake Tanganyika, engraved with the words 'WAIT HERE FOR THE MALLARD EXPEDITION'.

Duck Tour leaving stone, I presume?

11th November

Forgot to put blueberries in the little cakes I sold at the big alpine slalom race today.

But it doesn't really matter in the grand ski muffins.

Also, I've been looking for my Russian settee. It's around here somewhere.

12th November

STILL looking for my Russian settee. So near and nyet sofa.

13th November

Tried playing 'Guess the first names of the Mr. Men' today.

But it wasn't Mike Uppity.

14th November

My pet snail just told me that he gets embarrassed about leaving a slimy trail.

And to be honest I can see where he's coming from.

15th November

I've started selling toasters from a hotel lobby.

It's pretty slow, but fortunately I've got a few irons in the foyer.

16th November

Just got sacked from my job making red Teletubby-branded refrigerated yurts because they didn't get cold enough.

It was only my first day.

Sadly I never realised my full Po tent chill.

17th November

Just found out I've been kicked out of Peripheral Vision Club.

I did NOT see that coming.

18th November

I think my grey hair might be limiting my earning potential.

I'm going to get rich or try dyeing.

19th November

Saw an Irish dancing show today called 'Streamdance'.

It's not as good at Riverdance, but it's a decent tributary act.

20th November

My son may have been expelled from school today for lifting the Principal in the air...

But at least he left with his Head held high.

21st November

My new job working in fungus identification is really dull.

Every day it's just say 'mould', say 'mould'...

22nd November

Bought some asparagus grown in Northern France today.

I don't know why they didn't call it 'Brittany Spears'.

23rd November

Bought a gemstone off Tom Jones today.

He couldn't tell me how old it was, but it's not a new jewel.

24th November

>Recently bought our chicken a cap with a bell on it.

>But I've managed to lose it today and I don't suppose I'll ever hear the hen doff it.

25th November

>Struggling with some admin today.

>The problem with trying to organise the Fight Club beer festival is no one wants to talk about the ale event in the room.

26th November

>Had to go to the dentist today.

>She asked how long I spend cleaning between my teeth each day.

>I never do, but said an hour because I wanted to make up flossed time.

27th November

>I've just painted myself with a limited-edition violet-blue colour for today's fun run.

>And now I'm rare indigo.

28th November

Got robbed today.

All I had on me was a defective set of scales, but they took it anyway.

I told them, "You'll never get a weigh with this!"

29th November

Never leave an auction room saying 'I bid you good day'. I know this now.

I ended up with a horrible vase and had to take the seller to a theme park.

30th November

Earlier my wife said she had secreted my biro somewhere in the house.

I said, "You've got a bic hidden!"

But she was serious.

DECEMBER

IF YOU WANT ME TO FLOAT TO THE GROUND, THAT'LL BE £100. AND I WON'T SETTLE FOR ANYTHING LESS...

@pauleggleston

1st December

Saw a mate today.

He said his wife is trying to make a beef stew SO hot that it warms the whole of the United Kingdom to the temperature at which a lightbulb will frazzle insects of the order Lepidoptera.

I said, "Heats bourguignon 'til UK hot like crisp moths?"

He said, "Yes. It is feeling rather festive, isn't it?"

2nd December

I saw this guy flag down a polecat today, on his way to meet a friend who happens to be a famous Icelandic singer.

He was whistling a Christmas song*.

*The ferret-hailer knew Bjork.

3rd December

The local umbrella depot has asked if I can install some access flaps so the mallards from the nearby pond can come in over the festive season, if they want.

Duck door holes, warehouse of brolly. Falalalala lalala LAAAA!

4th December

Today I saw a vision of the Roman Goddess of wisdom, carved from citrus wood, surrounded by an expanse of crunchy lichen.

She told me that it's going to snow on the 25th December.

Lime tree Minerva, wide crisp moss. Just like the ones I used to know.

5th December

Just came home to find some little blue creatures roasting on an open fire.

It's beginning to look a lot like crisp Smurfs.

6th December

Went to the panto today. They had a statue of Cinderella there.

I didn't like it, but I found the plinth charming.

7th December

I wanted to check my wife's knowledge of trivia, so I asked if she had a quiz mastery.

Apparently we both do!

It's being delivered tomorrow, and it's a Norway Spruce.

8th December

Just remembered how one of the great soul singers once sent me a festive garland, just to annoy me.

It was a wreath of rankling.

9th December

I've got my wife a limited-edition bottle of Tippex for Christmas.

It's a corrector's item.

10th December

Just had that recurring dream that I always get in the winter.

I dreamt that I was a badger.

I woke up in a cold sett.

11th December

The seabird that lives in our rubbish keeps causing a nuisance by applying hair styling products whilst squawking a Christmas song.

He got two warnings from the police before they arrested him today.

Bin Gull gels, Bin Gull gels, Bin Gull hauled away.

12th December

Someone just came through on my walkie talkie, out of breath, claiming to be one of Santa's helpers.

Yeah I'll believe that when Elf wheezes 'OVER'..!

13th December

Just written my name on my 'All I Want For Christmas Is My Two Front Teeth' single.

Just in case I ever need to be identified by my dental records.

14th December

Last Christmas
I gave my wife a book entitled 'Cure your obsession with how heavy your gifts are'.
But the very next day
She gave it a weigh.

15th December

Starting a new job today, at the local dog track. It's only temporary, while the weather is cold.

My main responsibility is stopping the greyhounds from freezing mid-race. I'm really hoping to grit the hound running.

16th December

I crave attention at Christmas, so I'm giving everyone sheets of pressed wool.

To make my presents felt.

17th December

Just realised that baby Jesus actually received two blocks of gold on his birth.

Making him the first child in history to have an Au pair.

18th December

My wife thinks that trying to get a sugar rush from stuffing my face with a selection of festive desserts all in one sitting is a terrible idea.

I suppose that's one wave pudding hit.

19th December

My wife said she was going to listen to a new Christmas album by that Canadian singer who, incidentally, had recently bought a bicycle that will tell him the weight of his bosoms.

I said, "Bike'll moob weigh?"

But apparently it was Bryan Adams.

20th December

My wife just asked why I'm pouring Domestos on our prickly plant.

But she definitely said 'tis the season to bleach holly.

21st December

I've decided that people who don't know what gum resin is need to get out myrrh.

22nd December

Works Christmas party today.

I had to tell a guy dressed as an enormous gorilla that he'd got cheese spread on his neckwear.

"King Kong!! Dairylea on tie!"

23rd December

Since I stopped taking that medication to reduce my stomach acid production my road rage has definitely improved.

I'm hardly beeping my horn at all. I was even singing along to a Christmas song* in the car earlier.

*Zantac loss is calming toot down.

24th December

Heard a whisper today that the wise men doubled up on one of their gifts.

Well I say whisper... it was actually more of a myrrh-myrrh.

25th December

Happy Christmas!

I was wondering why the Innkeeper didn't offer up his cabin used for storing dried petals & spices for the virgin birth.

But on reflection it would have been holy in a potpourri hut.

26th December

I've just invented a miniature rollercoaster that's exactly the same width as one of the digits on my dominant hand.

It's a right knuckle wide!

27th December

That 'If I Could Turn Back Time' singer has been in Sherwood Forest stealing prosciutto-wrapped almonds from the rich and giving them to the poor. Who does she think she is?

Robin Hood? Or the...

Cher offer nut in ham?

28th December

I can never remember which calendar era Michael Jackson most liked to sing about.

It was either A)BC or B)AD.

29th December

It's the 'Rear of the Year' awards tonight.

I don't like to brag, but I've won it for the last two years running.

I would say I'm hoping to win it a third time, but that would be Arse King for treble.

30th December

Already got going with my new year's resolution of not singing that Celine Dion song off Titanic.

I've started as I mean to.. GO ONNNNN. Dammit.

31st December

New Year's Eve!!!

But as we remember the younger ordinary ants tonight, we should all spare a thought for the older quaint ants being forgot.

ABOUT THE AUTHOR

Paul Eggleston is a comedy writer, specialising in the most tortuous and convoluted puns (a style which he has developed over the years on Twitter) but regularly turns his hand to pithier one liners too, and the occasional cartoon.

He was once named as one of the 100 funniest people on Twitter (by 'The Poke') but we won't dwell on how long ago that was.

Paul lives in Suffolk with his wife and two children. Oh, and Cookie and Crumble too, of course.

You can follow Paul on Twitter at @paaleggleston

WHAT THEY'RE SAYING ON TWITTER:

'Possibly THE best joke writer on Twitter'

'A wonderfully skewed mind'

'A true master of the genre... like wonderfully intricate puzzles you have to solve'

'A man obsessed with the notion of going so far out of his way to force a pun that the journey back becomes not just worth it, but often surpasses the gag'

'The best multi-word pun master on Twitter'

'Everyone follow this bloke, he just made darjeeling shoot out of my nose'

'Never snidey, never nasty, but always rip-roaringly hilarious. Embodies all the best that Twitter can be...'

'A merciless and unrelenting punster, who manipulates words to do his unnatural bidding'

'Like playing scrabble with aliens in your dreams, and winning' *(I don't really understand this one, but I like it)*

'The pun equivalent to a cryptic crossword'

'Shouldn't be let loose on an unsuspecting public'

'No, God please, No! No! No!'

Printed in Great Britain
by Amazon